# Managing sickness absence and return to work

An employers' and managers' guide

HSE Books

© Crown copyright 2004

First published 2004

ISBN 0 7176 2882 5

All rights reserved. No part of this publication may be reproduced, stored in a retrieval system, or transmitted in any form or by any means (electronic, mechanical, photocopying, recording or otherwise) without the prior written permission of the copyright owner.

Applications for reproduction should be made in writing to: Licensing Division, Her Majesty's Stationery Office, St Clements House, 2-16 Colegate, Norwich NR3 1BQ or by e-mail to hmsolicensing@cabinet-office.x.gsi.gov.uk

Most of the text in this booklet is intended to simply provide practical information. Where reference is made to relevant legal duties this should not be regarded as an authoritative statement of the law and for legal advice readers should refer, in the first instance, to the sources signposted in Appendices 5 and 6.

# Contents

| | |
|---|---|
| Preface | v |
| Foreword | vii |
| Steps to manage sickness absence and return to work | viii |
| **Introduction** | 1 |
| Why is this guidance relevant to me? | 1 |
| How will this guide help me? | 1 |
| Terms used in the guide | 1 |
| **Understanding the employer's role** | 3 |
| Isn't management of sickness absence best left to medical people? | 3 |
| Do I have any legal responsibilities to help ill, injured or disabled employees back to work? | 3 |
| **Managing return to work** | 5 |
| When are employees likely to need help? | 5 |
| What does managing return to work involve? | 5 |
| **Recording sickness absence** | 6 |
| How do I use sickness absence data to manage return to work? | 6 |
| Do I have data protection responsibilities? | 6 |
| **Keeping in contact** | 7 |
| Dos and don'ts for keeping in contact | 7 |
| When and how often should contact be made? | 7 |
| Getting the tone right | 8 |
| What if my absent employee refuses contact? | 8 |
| Conducting a return to work interview | 9 |
| I suspect my employee has a health problem but they are not absent | 9 |
| What if my employee becomes distressed? | 9 |
| **Planning and undertaking workplace adjustments** | 10 |
| Why do I need to make adjustments? | 10 |
| Becoming disability-aware | 10 |
| How do I find out about what adjustments are needed? | 10 |
| Making reasonable adjustments | 11 |
| Examples of reasonable adjustments | 11 |
| Meeting health and safety requirements | 12 |
| What if my employee cannot return to their original job? | 13 |
| Employment rights | 14 |
| **Making use of professional or other advice and treatment** | 15 |
| When might professional or other advice be needed? | 15 |
| Using professional advice from occupational health and rehabilitation services, insurers and others | 15 |
| Helping with prompt provision of treatment | 16 |
| Taxable benefits | 16 |
| How can I get help with reasonable adjustments for disabled employees? | 17 |
| What if my employee's ill health is caused by conflicts at work? | 18 |
| **Agreeing and reviewing a return to work plan** | 19 |
| Agreeing a return to work plan | 19 |
| When is the right time to prepare a plan? | 19 |
| Who should put the plan together? | 19 |
| What needs to go into the plan? | 19 |
| Putting the plan into operation | 20 |
| **Co-ordinating the return to work process** | 21 |
| When might a co-ordinator be necessary? | 21 |
| Using a case manager | 21 |
| **Developing a policy on return to work and putting it into practice** | 22 |
| Do I need to develop a policy? | 22 |
| How do I go about preparing a policy statement? | 22 |
| Helping your line managers and supervisors to support the policy | 23 |
| Welcoming returning employees back | 23 |
| Promoting awareness and understanding of disability and ill health | 23 |
| **Appendix 1** Relevant legislation | 24 |
| **Appendix 2** GP advice on returning to work | 27 |
| **Appendix 3** Employers' liability insurance (ELCI/ELDECI) | 28 |
| **Appendix 4** Suggested content of a return to work policy | 29 |
| **Appendix 5** Organisations that can provide further advice | 31 |
| **Appendix 6** Useful publications | 36 |
| **References** | 39 |

# Preface

Long-term sickness absence represents a significant burden on both employers and employees in the public and private sectors. It involves a relatively small number of people, but has a huge cost. All too often the outcome for employers is mounting sick pay, reduced productivity and unnecessary recruitment and for employees, reduced earnings, job loss for some and an increased workload for colleagues.

Such wastage is not inevitable. Actions taken in the early stages of sickness absence can result in an early return to work and be more cost-effective than bringing in somebody new. I want all of Government to work together with employers to ensure that everyone who can work is helped to do so. I therefore welcome this best practice resource that HSE has put together which offers employers and managers simple, practical and proactive steps to help employees following injury, ill health or the onset of disability, to return to work. By following these we can reduce sickness absence, improve the competitiveness and productivity of our businesses and protect the well-being of employees.

RT HON JANE KENNEDY MP
MINISTER OF STATE FOR WORK

# Foreword

The Health and Safety Commission's strategy for workplace health and safety in Great Britain indicates our determination to promote partnerships to help workers stay healthy and in work.

We know that long-term sickness has a devastating effect on the productivity of business and the well-being and employment prospects of workers. We believe employers working with trade union and other employee representatives can do much to prevent injury and ill health in the first place, ensure that sickness absence is properly managed and help employees return to their jobs. We recognise employers need support, advice and encouragement to tackle these issues. I therefore commend this best practice guide, which brings together evidence from independent experts, the experience of a wide range of stakeholders and HSE's expertise in promoting safe and healthy workplaces. If we meet this challenge there are gains for employees and employers.

I would like to thank all those who have helped in developing this guide by organising and attending discussion forums, giving advice and providing case studies.

*Bill Callaghan*

BILL CALLAGHAN
CHAIR, HEALTH AND SAFETY COMMSSION

# Steps to manage sickness absence and return to work

This chart shows the steps you and your business can take, in partnership with your employees, to manage sickness absence and help employees to get back to work, to the benefit of everyone. It also gives a general guide to the time frame for carrying out the action described.

The chart is intended as a memory aid and directs you to the relevant paragraphs in the main text of the guide.

# Introduction

## Why is this guidance relevant to me?

1  Sickness absence can have a big impact on the productivity of your business and the life of your employees. This booklet guides you through the process of helping ill, injured or disabled employees on long-term sick leave to return to their jobs as soon as possible. Its contents will also be of interest to trade union and other employee representatives.

2  Everyone at work will probably need to take sick leave at some time during their working lives and in most cases this only lasts a few days. But if absence is prolonged it can have devastating effects on your business costs and the quality of life of the employee concerned.

3  Work, provided it is managed safely and effectively, is essential to good health and well-being (see References). Inability to get back to work due to poor health brings on more health problems, both physical and mental (see References). The longer people are off work, the less likely it is that they will return. Research shows that after only six weeks' sickness absence, a person's ability to return to work falls away rapidly. Almost one in five people who reach this point will stay off work sick and eventually leave paid employment.

4  But this journey is not inevitable and you can take action to prevent the loss of your employees through poor health. If you do this you will:

- avoid unnecessary recruitment and training expenditure and maintain competitiveness in a full employment economy;
- reduce your Statutory Sick Pay (SSP) and overall sickness absence costs;
- avoid significant penalties for discriminating against disabled workers;
- improve workplace relations;
- raise your organisation's reputation;
- safeguard the livelihood of your employees, and so benefit their families and communities.

Companies in both the UK and USA have made significant savings by introducing return to work programmes (see References).

## How will this guide help me?

5  This guide sets out good practice, with examples, for managing sickness absence and return to work in partnership with trade union and other employee representatives. It covers all absence due to ill health, injury or disability whether or not it is related to work. In particular, it:

- takes you through the steps to helping people back to work;
- provides advice on workplace and external factors that can act as barriers to successful return to work;
- offers suggestions on developing a company or organisational return to work policy;
- gives advice on preventing risks to the health and safety of ill, injured or disabled employees;
- summarises relevant legislation;
- lists other sources of help and information.

6  The guide does not set out to provide detailed advice on the following topics but does help you to find more information about them (see the organisations and publications listed in Appendices 5 and 6):

- the occasions when disciplinary action may be necessary as part of absence management;
- employment rights and contractual obligations;
- statutory sick pay and related state allowances and benefits;
- recruiting disabled people or people in poorer health into work for the first time, or after long-term unemployment, although some of the advice given will be relevant to these situations.

## Terms used in the guide

*Rehabilitation and return to work*
7  The process of helping employees return to work and regain their capacity following illness or injury, or to adjust to disability at work is often called 'occupational rehabilitation' or 'vocational rehabilitation'. Such terms are well understood by occupational health and other medical professionals. But for many employees the word 'rehabilitation' has a variety of different meanings, not all of which are related to work. Employees who are helped to return to work after illness may not see themselves as being 'rehabilitated'. This guide refers to return or readjustment to work, as far as possible, instead of 'rehabilitation'.

Introduction

### *Long-term absence*
8   In this guide, the words 'long-term absence' are generally used to mean absences of more than four weeks. It is at this point that the risk of not returning to work starts to grow. But there are certain actions, like keeping in contact with absent employees, that will need to be taken before this milestone is reached (see paragraph 30), so that you are ready to respond appropriately if your employee remains off sick.

### *Trade union and other employee representatives*
9   It is possible that you may not have trade union representatives at your workplace, but if there are such representatives it is essential that you involve them in agreeing your procedures for helping employees return to work. Where return to work involves health and safety issues you are legally required to discuss the matter with trade union safety representatives or if there are none, other employee representatives (see paragraphs 10-13 in Appendix 1). But the return to work process involves matters where the experience of any trade union equality and disability representatives at the workplace, as well as employees themselves, will be useful.

# Understanding the employer's role

## Isn't management of sickness best left to medical people?

10 No. Getting back to work is part of the process of recovering from ill health or adjusting to disability and employers have a vital role to play. Practical steps like allowing an employee to come back on the basis of shortened hours for a limited period can make an earlier and successful return more likely. Surprisingly, the majority of people who leave work through ill health do not do so because of severe illness. Most suffer from common health complaints experienced by many of us, like mild to moderate mental health problems, or muscle, joint or back pain. Their inability to get back to work points to the existence of problems that health care alone does not solve. Recent research reflects growing recognition that overcoming social and other non-medical, especially work-related, barriers is key to whether an absent employee returns to work following illness, injury or the onset of disability (see References).

11 Using good practice to help employees return to work after sickness absence and stay in post need not be difficult. It goes hand in hand with good people management, and effective health and safety management. You may already have a number of the building blocks in place. Getting started on good practice will usually mean taking a fresh look at the ways in which:

- you work with trade union and other employee representatives on help for ill, injured or disabled workers;
- you check and record sickness absence;
- your managers are trained to deal with sickness absence and disability;
- you involve absent employees in planning their return to work;
- wage arrangements and conditions of work can help or hinder return;
- you plan reasonable adjustments for disabled workers;
- you control any risks to employees from work activities;
- work is managed to prevent poor health being made worse by work.

All these examples are discussed in more detail in this guide.

12 There is also action that employees themselves can take to help you make their return easier. HSE has published a free employees' leaflet called *Off work sick and worried about your job? Steps you can take to help your return to work* (see Appendix 6 for details of this and other HSE publications on sickness absence).

13 The guide encourages a high standard of cooperation and partnership between employers, employees, and trade union and other employee representatives. Open and constructive discussion and co-operation between the parties is vital to the successful management of sickness absence and return to work. Agreeing a return to work policy, as set out later in this guide, can only benefit your business (see paragraphs 21 and 97-103).

## Do I have any legal responsibility to help ill, injured or disabled employees back to work?

14 There is no law that requires you to assist every ill or injured employee in your workforce to return to work. But disabled employees are protected by the Disability Discrimination Act (DDA) 1995 (see paragraphs 46-49 in the main text and 14-19 in Appendix 1) which means that you do have to make reasonable adjustments to their working conditions or arrangements to make sure that they are not treated less favourably than other employees. Employees whose injury or poor health persists may become eligible for DDA protection.

15 You also have responsibilities under the Health and Safety at Work etc Act 1974 (HSWA) or in Northern Ireland (NI), Health and Safety at Work etc Order 1978 (HSWO), and related legislation, to protect employees, after they return to work, if they have become more vulnerable to risk because of illness, injury or disability. In practice, compliance with these duties takes time and can often be made easier by taking action in consultation with employees and their representatives before they return.

16 This guide sets out ways you can avoid unnecessary dismissals and retirements due to ill health, but if you consider taking such action, remember that you have responsibilities under the:

- Employment Rights Act 1996 (NI Employment Rights Order 1996) to adopt fair procedures before dismissing employees on grounds of sickness absence; and the
- Employment Act 2002 (NI Employment Order 2003) to adopt statutory minimum dismissal, disciplinary and grievance procedures (these come into force in October 2004).

Understanding the employer's role

17  The responsibilities outlined in paragraphs 14-16 are summarised in Appendix 1. Further information is available from the organisations and publications listed in Appendices 5 (in particular, items 2-15) and 6.

18  Bear in mind also the company's or organisation's contractual obligations to your employee and theirs to you to abide by their contract of employment, unless there are lawful reasons for them not to do so.

# Managing return to work

## When are employees likely to need help?

19  Employees who may need your help and support to stay at work include people:

- who become ill or injured and whose job performance could be affected if their condition gets worse;
- already in poor health, or experiencing stress, whose condition might be made worse unless the system of working is changed;
- whose condition already affects their job performance and may begin to affect their attendance;
- whose condition has resulted in long-term absence who need help to return;
- who become disabled as defined by the DDA (see paragraphs 15-18 in Appendix 1).

20  Employees to whom the first three bullets in paragraph 19 apply, also risk entering the fourth unless someone intervenes to help them. People at particular risk are those with common health problems for which there is no clear medical diagnosis. Often it is work-related barriers that prevent their return and you can help them to overcome these.

## What does managing return to work involve?

21  There are six elements in the return to work process:

- recording sickness absence (paragraphs 22-27);
- keeping in contact with sick employees, including return to work interviews (paragraphs 28-43);
- planning and undertaking workplace controls or adjustments to help workers on sickness absence to return and stay in work (paragraphs 44-69);
- making use of professional advice and treatment (paragraphs 70-82);
- agreeing and reviewing a return to work plan (paragraphs 83-92);
- co-ordinating the return to work process (paragraphs 93-96).

You may find it helpful to set out a company or organisational approach to these elements, termed a 'policy' in this guide (paragraphs 97-107).

# Recording sickness absence

## How do I use sickness absence data to manage return to work?

22  You need to keep records for statutory sick pay purposes, but knowing who among your employees is off sick and why is also essential information for:

- identifying employees whose return may be delayed or prevented unless you intervene;
- helping employees whose frequent absences may disguise other, eg domestic problems;
- planning cover for the absent employee's work;
- checking for patterns of ill health that could highlight possible work-related causes, or the onset of disability;
- benchmarking your performance against your competitors to judge whether your own record is good or bad.

For further advice on SSP contact the Inland Revenue (see item 25 in Appendix 5) or refer to their publications listed in Appendix 6.

23  If your organisation is very small you will be well aware of who is off sick at any one time. But it is still important to know why they are sick in case the cause could be work related or adjustments are necessary to help them return. In larger organisations, analysis of sickness absence records can reveal patterns of illness or injury that could be caused by or made worse by work, eg:

- a number of cases of back, joint or muscle pain amongst employees who carry out a particular task;
- frequent minor but vague illness in areas where deadlines are very tight, workloads are challenging or employees have little control over their work.

24  Early action on your part can increase the chances of a quicker return to work significantly. Recording sickness absence daily and summing it up on a weekly basis will help keep the information accurate and prompt you to make contact with absent employees at suitable intervals. Reporting cases of work-related injury or ill health to your insurers, as early as possible, increases the possibility of helping employees affected to return to work (see also Appendix 3).

25  The suggested minimum information that you will need to help you manage absence and return to work, some of which you already keep for SSP purposes, is the:

- name or identification of the employee concerned and where they can be contacted;
- date of the first day of absence;
- cause of absence;
- whether the injury or illness is considered to be work related, once this is known;
- working days absent (updated regularly);
- date employee last contacted and the outcome;
- expected length of absence, if known;
- return to work date.

26  HSE is currently developing a straightforward, web-based format for recording and monitoring sickness absence. For further information go to HSE's website (see item 14 of Appendix 5).

## Do I have data protection responsibilities?

27  The sickness absence data that you keep has to comply with the Data Protection Act 1998. If an absence record contains specific medical information relating to an employee, this is deemed as sensitive data and you will have to satisfy the statutory conditions for processing such data. For further advice see item 1 of Appendix 5 on contacting the Information Commissioner's Office and ICO publications also listed in Appendix 6.

# Keeping in contact

## Dos and don'ts for keeping in contact

28  Keeping in contact with absent employees is a key factor in helping them return after long-term absence. The line manager, the supervisor, or a human resources manager usually undertakes contact, but see the **dos and don'ts** below for more advice on the best person for this. Contact can be a sensitive topic as some employees may fear that they will be pressed to come back to work before they are ready. But without contact, employees who have been absent for some weeks may feel increasingly out of touch and undervalued. Physical and mental health can become worse, the employee loses self-esteem and their return is made more difficult for them and for you.

29  On the other hand, you or your line managers may feel nervous about getting enough information from absent employees to plan absence cover and action to help them return, without appearing intrusive. Similarly you may feel uncomfortable about talking to an employee whose performance, combined with frequent short-term absence, is causing you concern. These are very real issues for which there are no hard and fast rules, but with the right approach you can handle them confidently. Listed below are some suggested **dos and don'ts** to help you deal with them. More advice about support and training for line managers and supervisors to help them deal with return to work issues is set out in paragraphs 103-104.

*Do*
- take time to know your employees and the things that affect their health, (or make sure your line managers or supervisors do so), as this will help you decide the kind of contact they would welcome;
- create a climate of trust by agreeing methods, frequency and reasons for keeping in contact, with your line managers and human resources managers, if any, and trade union or other employee representatives;
- consider training for yourself, your managers and your employees on a sensitive approach to helping each other get the most out of contact;
- consider the timing and form of contacts, and who should make them;
- take advice from the employees' colleagues, human resources managers or trade union and other employee representatives if you are unsure how to make contact;
- be flexible, treat each case individually, but on a fair and consistent basis;
- encourage discussion, particularly with trade union or other employee representatives about overcoming barriers to return;
- if the employee is able to travel, suggest they come in to see colleagues at lunch time or during coffee breaks;
- keep a note of contacts made;
- welcome the employee back to work after their absence;
- carry out return to work interviews;
- give employees the opportunity to discuss their health or other concerns that are affecting their performance or attendance in private;
- remember that medication can have side effects on things like physical stamina, mood, driving, machinery operation and safety critical tasks.

*Don't*
- wait until someone goes on long-term absence to consider your contact strategy, but plan ahead in partnership with your management team and trade union and employee representatives;
- put off making contact or pass responsibility to someone else unless there are sound reasons for doing so;
- make assumptions about the employee's situation or their medical circumstances;
- talk to other people about the employee's circumstances without that person's knowledge and consent;
- put pressure on employees to discuss their return before they are ready;
- say that colleagues or teammates are under pressure or that work is piling up;
- forget that recovery times for the same condition can vary significantly from person to person.

In the case of mental health, there is a useful line managers' resource guide available via the National Institute for Mental Health in England (see the publications list in Appendix 6) that includes keeping in contact with absent employees.

## When and how often should contact be made?

30  Each case needs to be treated individually. When employees notify minor illness that is likely to end within or just after the self-certification period of seven days, further contact, except for certification purposes, is not usually necessary. But a return to work interview (see paragraphs 39-41) will be useful to get people back up to speed or discuss underlying causes if such absence is frequent. In circumstances of traumatic injury or sudden serious illness, extend your sympathies and use discretion until the longer

term prognosis becomes clearer. Employees undergoing planned treatment may welcome hospital visits, particularly if you contact relatives first. If you are notified that employees are suffering from depression or a stress-related illness it is normally good practice to make contact within a week to show the organisation's concern for them, (see References) but they are unlikely to be ready to discuss returning at this stage. Generally, it is advisable to contact sick employees as early as possible and certainly before 14 days go by.

31  If the employee is being treated at home, you may need to discuss with relatives or other carers the best time to make contact. First contacts will normally be by phone. It may be helpful to try to make home visits firstly for welfare reasons and then, at the right time to help plan for return to work. Such visits should be carefully prepared with the employees' consent and in liaison with relatives or other appropriate people, eg trade union and other employee representatives, human resources or occupational health professionals, welfare officers and employee assistance providers.

## Getting the tone right

32  If you have discussed absence management with your employees and their trade union and other employee representatives in an open and constructive way, employees who are absent will understand that you need to use these contacts to:

- assess what help you can provide, including reasonable adjustments in the case of disabled employees;
- find out when they will be able to return;
- get information to help you plan cover for their work in their absence;
- explain pay rates for their absence;
- check their understanding of your absence management procedures.

33  Make sure your conversation with the absent employee is clearly focused on their well-being and their return to work. Try to focus as much on what the employee can do as things they may need help with. Returning to work is an important milestone in getting life back on track, but if the employee is made to feel a 'problem' in some way, they will feel disheartened. Absent employees can be encouraged to talk to their own doctor, or other healthcare adviser about what they may be able to do as they make progress or adjust to their condition. This will help you to judge whether a gradual return may be the best way forward or whether other reasonable adjustments are more appropriate (see paragraphs 44-61 for information on reasonable adjustments).

34  A vital aspect of keeping in contact is helping your employee stay tuned into work and the workplace. Keep them up to date with news, both informal and formal, about teammates and the workplace. They may appreciate copies of newsletters or circulars.

35  Unwelcome news, such as a reduction in pay due to continuing absence, needs to be delivered sensitively, stressing your continuing concern to help them back to work if you can. Avoid unpleasant surprises by making sure that all employees, including new starters, are familiar with your absence management procedures, including pay rates for long-term absence and when disciplinary procedures might apply.

## What if my absent employee refuses contact?

36  Make sure your employees understand their responsibility to keep you informed of the reasons why they are absent from the work for which they are employed and, when known, how long the absence is likely to last. Your company or organisational rules need to set out clearly when and how to notify absence.

37  But employee reluctance to notify illness or keep in contact may be connected to issues that require sensitive handling. The employee may feel embarrassed about describing their condition. Other examples include illness related to difficult working relationships with managers or others, bullying, harassment or heavy workload. Ways of dealing with these in the short term, depending on the severity of the problem include:

- making sure the employee knows who they can talk to other than their manager, eg a human resources manager, or occupational health provider, if any;
- using trade union or other employee representatives as intermediaries, especially if there is an established bond of trust between the employee and the representative;
- enabling the employee to talk to someone of the same sex or religion, or at a neutral place, away from work and home;
- making first contact in writing, offering help with any problems at work;
- using an independent mediator (see paragraph 82).

38 If bullying or harassment proves to be the issue, you will need to tackle the root of the problem in partnership with trade union and other employee representatives. Staff need to understand that bullying is never acceptable and that sexual, racial and disability harassment are illegal (see paragraph 19 in Appendix 1).

## Conducting a return to work interview

39 Interviewing your employee on their return to work gives you both an opportunity to confirm that the record of sickness absence is accurate and discuss any remaining health concerns that may affect work. This can range from an informal chat to establish that your employee is sufficiently recovered from minor illness to putting the final touches to the return to work plan. It is also an opportunity to discuss any reasonable adjustments to work needed if the employee has a disability. The main thing is to listen well and be objective. The employee may wish to have a trade union representative or other employee representative present. Remember to ensure that the interview is accessible for disabled employees in terms of venue, language (for people with learning difficulties), and provision of support or equipment.

40 Frequent short-term absences for minor illness may mask worsening health, or stressful situations at work, abuse of alcohol or drugs or difficulties at home. These can lead to poor performance and more serious illness leading to longer absences if nothing is done. A sensitive and non-judgemental approach can help bring out any underlying problems. Ask questions, that cannot be answered by 'yes' or 'no' alone, about how they are feeling, how long any problems (inside or outside work) have been going on, whether others feel the same.

This guide does not address drug or alcohol abuse but see the HSE and HSENI leaflets in Appendix 6 for sources of advice on these problems.

41 If stress at work is the problem, introduce controls to prevent harmful pressure building up. If balancing work and domestic demands are contributing to illness, consider what help, appropriate to the size of your business and its resources, you can offer to employees to help balance work and home demands, eg a change in shift pattern, flexible hours or working from home, or encouragement to contact employee assistance counselling services, if provided, or external advisory agencies.

## I suspect my employee has a health problem but they are not absent

42 If your employee's performance or productivity has decreased for no apparent reason or they are behaving out of character, they may be unwell or reacting to pressure of some kind. Take advantage of performance appraisals, or other private discussions to talk through any concerns they may have using the principles in paragraphs 39-41. See whether they would like to talk to your occupational health adviser, if you have one. If you find out that your employee has become disabled, discuss with them whether reasonable adjustments are needed to accommodate their situation. It may be useful to agree a plan of action similar to that in paragraphs 89-90.

## What if my employee becomes distressed?

43 No matter how carefully you discuss health, disability or absence problems there may be times when your employee becomes distressed. If this happens, stay focused, give them time to recover and reassure them you are listening. Find out whether they are aware of sources of support and help them as necessary. Arrange another meeting if appropriate, but do recognise that that there may be limits to what you can deal with personally and to the details which employees feel comfortable in discussing. In these circumstances referral to counselling, occupational health or other professional support services may be appropriate. You or your managers may need training and support to deal with tragic circumstances or severe illness.

# Planning and undertaking workplace adjustments

## Why do I need to make adjustments?

44  Keeping in contact with employees while they are absent will help you plan any adjustments to their work that may be needed for their return. Planning action with your employee will help them feel closer to the goal of getting back as soon as is appropriate. Some adjustments may also be necessary to enable employees with illnesses that could worsen over time to stay in post.

45  In general terms, the purpose of adjustments is to:

- return the employee to their existing job with such modifications as are needed, or to an alternative one if there are no adjustments that would make this possible;
- retain valuable skills;
- remove the problems or barriers that would otherwise make return to work difficult.

Examples of adjustments are given in paragraph 60.

## Becoming disability-aware

46  If the employee is or becomes disabled, you are legally required under the Disability Discrimination Act (DDA) 1995 to make reasonable adjustments to enable the employee to continue working. It does not follow that all disabled people will need permanent adjustments to help them work, many will not. But if an individual does need such help, you need to make sure that you do all you reasonably can to modify their job, including access to it, and/or their working arrangements. What is reasonable will depend on:

- the financial and other impact of modifications on your business and its activities;
- how effective modifications are likely to be;
- the particular needs of the individual employee, not the nature of their disability alone; and
- the availability of financial or other assistance for the employer (eg the Access to Work (AtW) Scheme).

If you are in any doubt about what might be reasonable, take advice from eg the Disability Rights Commission (see the contact details in item 4 of Appendix 5) or their publications also listed in Appendix 6).

47  The purpose of the DDA is to protect and prevent discrimination against people defined as having physical or mental impairments which have a substantial (ie more than minor or trivial) and long-term effect on their ability to carry out normal day-to-day activities. Examples of impairments are set out in paragraphs 16-18 of Appendix 1.

48  If you know that an employee is disabled (see paragraph 53) then you have a duty to comply with the DDA. But disability is not always a clear-cut issue. The DDA covers some conditions that you cannot readily 'see' like diabetes, for which no adjustments may be necessary unless there are additional factors. By contrast, someone in pain may not be disabled under the DDA, but may need help to return. But if an everyday mental or physical condition persists in the longer term the person concerned may become disabled under the DDA.

49  The adjustments needed by an employee following illness or injury and those necessary for a disabled person will often be similar. It is helpful to get into the habit of considering reasonable adjustments to help an employee return whether or not they are disabled in the legal sense.

## How do I find out about what adjustments are needed?

50  Adjustments need not be difficult. You can often find solutions by working together with your employee and with trade union and other employee representatives without external advice. But there will be times when it is helpful to have professional advice (see paragraphs 70-82).

51  The key steps in planning adjustments are:

- in discussion with your employee, forming a view of their needs and capability;
- seeking professional advice, when necessary, to help you and your employee make informed decisions;
- assessing the possible barriers to their return;
- considering, with trade union or other employee representatives, the modifications or adjustments needed to overcome the barriers;
- reviewing health and safety risk assessments in the light of the proposed modifications;
- reviewing how well the modifications or adjustments work.

52  Start by gathering information from the employee concerned about the kind of help they might need to get back to work. Remember that information about an employee's health should not be revealed to teammates, colleagues or trade union and other employee representatives unless you have the informed consent of the employee concerned. Your task will be made much easier if

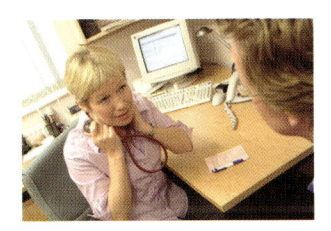

you have established a climate of trust. Employees need to be confident that any information they give you will not be shared inappropriately or used against them. The information you might wish to discuss with your employee may include:

- what would help them to return and what would hinder them, eg would anything about the job or the hours of work need to be changed or modified?
- any side effects of ongoing treatment or medication which could affect work;
- a rough estimate of when return to work might be possible;
- whether they have discussed returning to work with their GP and any advice they have been given about returning to work (see also Appendix 2 on the role of GPs);
- further information which a specialist, eg an occupational health practitioner, may need to give.

53  In some businesses, such information will be gathered by an occupational health adviser. Your adviser should alert you if your employee is disabled under the DDA and is entitled to reasonable adjustments, but you may also need to act appropriately if you learn this from any other source. You may be in breach of the DDA if you or your advisers know of an employee's disability but fail to make any necessary reasonable adjustments.

## Making reasonable adjustments

54  Use the experience of the employee concerned, their teammates and trade union or other employee representatives to help you identify reasonable adjustments. This will of course need to give appropriate regard to the employee's right for privacy for health and personal information.

55  If an employee is suffering from back or joint pain, you may need to consider adjustments to ergonomic factors like working posture, use of muscle force for gripping and handling, the type of equipment used, the working environment, the pace of production and the spacing of rest breaks.

56  For some people with mental health conditions, appropriate adjustments may include building up to normal workloads over a period of time, and regular meetings with line managers and colleagues to support and encourage the employee. It is important to talk to the employee concerned about the kind of support and adjustments they may need and take expert advice if necessary.

57  If the mental health condition arises from stress at work you will need to review the management system and how it could be altered to avoid pressures building up. Suitable training could help you with this. HSE has published advice on managing work-related stress and on your legal duties. This will help you find out if you have a problem with stress in the workplace and develop solutions (see the HSE publications listed in Appendix 6).

58  Do avoid making stereotypical assumptions about the capabilities of disabled people. These are unfounded and illegal. In fact, many people's disabilities have no impact on their job. As few as 4% of disabled people of working age need additional aids or health-related treatment that would interfere with working. The best advice will come from the people themselves, their GPs or disability employment services, disability charities and trade union equality or disability representatives.

59  Ill health or injury is sometimes traceable to a specific event in or out of the workplace such as an accident, excessive lifting, acute or regular exposure to hazardous substances, or traumatic occasions. Much more often it results from a combination of factors such as increased workloads, lack of control over work, failure to take breaks, or pressures and activities outside work. Pain and discomfort feel more acute when there are other difficulties to deal with at the same time, so it pays to consider the job in the round. For instance in the case of back pain, consider management and work systems as well as working positions, awkward movements and seating. Employees will readjust more easily and gain confidence to cope with, eg lingering pain, or depression brought about by events outside work, if they feel supported at work, demands are reasonable and tasks are satisfying.

## Examples of reasonable adjustments

60  Here are some examples of adjustments. They could be introduced temporarily while the employee regains strength, mobility or capacity to work, or they could form reasonable adjustments on a permanent basis to allow disabled employees to continue to work.

### Adjustments to working arrangements
- Allow a phased return to work to build up strength, eg building up from part-time to full-time hours over a period of weeks (see paragraph 61).
- Change individuals' working hours to allow travel at quieter times, or allow flexible working to ease their

work-life balance.
- Provide help with transport to and from work, eg organising lifts to work or for a disabled employee, finding out what help may be available to them through the AtW Scheme.
- Arrange home working (providing a safe working environment can be maintained).
- Allow the employee to be absent during working hours for rehabilitation assessment or treatment.

*Adjustments to premises*
- Move tasks to more accessible areas and closer to washing and toilet facilities.
- Make alterations to premises, eg providing a ramp for people who find steps difficult, improving lighting where sight-impaired employees work, providing clear visual signs and alerts for deaf employees.

*Adjustments to the job*
- Provide new or modify existing equipment and tools, including IT, modified keyboards etc.
- Modify workstations, furniture, movement patterns.
- Provide additional training for employees to do their job, eg refresher courses.
- Modify instructions or reference manuals.
- Modify work patterns or management systems and styles to reduce pressures and give the employee more control.
- Arrange telephone conferences to reduce travel, or if face-to-face meetings cause anxiety.
- Modify procedures for testing or assessment.
- Provide a buddy or mentor to your employee while they gain confidence back at work.
- Provide supervision.
- Reallocate work within the employee's team.
- Provide alternative work.

*Phased return*
61  In many cases of illness a phased or gradual return to normal hours within a fixed timescale is a key element of getting employees back to work before the barriers to return start building up. There is no single pattern that suits everyone, so agree one with your employee that works for both of you. Examples could involve:

- working four hours a day for one or more weeks, then six hours for two weeks, aiming for a full shift after about six weeks; or
- working up from one or two days a week.

Before coming to a decision, discuss with your employee

**Case study**
Paula was employed as a customer service assistant for a provincial newspaper when she was involved in a motorcycle accident on a day off. Her injuries meant she needed a wheelchair. Hers was a desk job dealing with customer queries, but it did involve her moving from office to office in a complex building. To enable Paula to return to work, her employer made adjustments to the glass panels in the doors on her routes at wheelchair height, changed the work surface area so that Paula's wheelchair could fit in and provided a suitable car parking space.

**Case study**
A Local Government Chief Officer returning after a prolonged period of mental illness was provided with a phased return and modified duties. In the first week back he attended for two half days, and then, over the following weeks, worked up to five full days in his seventh week. Full pay was reinstated from the first day back. He was given a role in which he used his professional expertise, but he did not take up day-to-day departmental management. His Chief Executive took him for lunch on the day before he returned, and on his first morning back he was greeted with a doughnuts and coffee 'party' attended by the Chief Executive and all his Divisional Managers. This arrangement was so successful in allowing him to readjust to work that it became the Council's standard for welcoming back any member of staff who was absent for a prolonged period.

(Acknowledgements to Employers' Organisation for local government *Management of Ill-Health Handbook*.)

what impact this will have on their pay. They may be better off delaying return until they are able to attend for, eg 50% of the time.

## Meeting health and safety requirements

62 Under health and safety law you have to undertake a risk assessment of your activities to prevent people being harmed by your work activities. Further information about these risk assessment requirements is set out in paragraphs 5-8 in Appendix 1 and in the HSE publications listed in Appendix 6. You need to review your risk assessment and possibly amend it:

- if there has been a significant change in your employee through illness, injury or disability that makes them vulnerable to additional risk; or
- if you are introducing adjustments as outlined in paragraphs 54-61 that could affect the work and health of others.

Normally the adjustments you put in place to help employees return should protect them from additional risk, but you may need to consider factors like the effects of medication in relation to driving or machinery operation or whether they could be more vulnerable to risk from potentially harmful substances, or agents such as vibration. You should also consider the impact on other employees if, eg work is reallocated.

63 You do not need to amend your risk assessment if existing control measures still offer your employee adequate protection or if additional measures would not offer increased protection. If your employee or others do face increased risk, amend the risk assessment and draw up an action list of the control measures you will introduce, and how they will be implemented. These measures should be reviewed as appropriate to make sure they are working effectively. The changes to the risk assessment and the action list must be discussed with the trade union safety or other employee representatives.

64 Everyone at work is entitled to the same standard of protection for their health and safety at work. Jumping to conclusions, without expert advice, about the impossibility of introducing controls that would enable disabled employees to stay at work would be discriminatory under the DDA. In most instances, health and safety responsibilities should not prove an insurmountable barrier to the retention of disabled workers. If a risk assessment suggests that it is not

**Case study**
Mary was employed as a support worker in an NHS Trust residential home for adults with learning difficulties when she was diagnosed as having diabetes. Staff working at the home are required to provide cover on a 24 hour basis which means one member of staff remaining awake throughout the night and another asleep, but on call.

Mary needs to be strict about her diet, blood sugar levels and medication. Doing the 'awake' shift would disrupt Mary's food intake and sleep patterns which could affect her blood sugar levels. If Mary did not do the 'awake' shifts then other members of the team would have to do more. The dilemma was discussed openly and Mary's managers and colleagues agreed that Mary would be 'excused' the 'awake' shifts but would take a greater share of the night 'sleep-in' and weekend day shifts. Mary, her colleagues and managers are happy with the arrangement.

**Case study**
L, a council caretaker, had been off work for 14 months with lower back pain, sciatica and subsequently circulatory problems in one leg. His occupational health nurse was aware that circulatory problems would take four to six months to sort out and in the meantime, he would be unable to act as caretaker. He was found a clerical job with the housing office in the area where he was based.

A more or less sedentary post was just what he needed while waiting for surgery. He felt that his IT skills, learnt from using a home computer, worked in his favour. However, his occupational health nurse was keen to emphasise that his temporary redeployment 'was also down to his attitude and determination'. L eventually returned to his caretaking job. However, he enjoyed his period as an office worker so much, he planned to apply to move permanently into this sort of work.

L felt the council, especially occupational health, handled his case very well. L's manager said: 'His case shows how you really do need to look at the individual, and to have a flexible approach that takes account of individual needs'.
(Acknowledgements to TUC *Rehabilitation and Retention Case Studies 2002*.)

reasonably practicable to reduce risks for a disabled worker to levels for other workers at your workplace:

- seek an open-minded assessment from a competent person who understands all the relevant issues;
- consult the disabled worker concerned;
- establish whether the excess risk amounts to one which is acceptable or one which is substantial and not reasonably practicable to overcome;
- discuss your findings with the employee concerned.

65  Trade union safety, and equality or disability representatives and other employee representatives have an important role in helping to identify risks and reasonably practicable ways of overcoming them. A reasonably practicable measure would be one that would not be grossly disproportionate to the cost of introducing it and the risk reduction it would achieve. Failure to retain an employee in order to protect their health and safety would only be justifiable if it could be shown that controlling the particular risks to the person concerned is not reasonably practicable.

### What if my employee cannot return to their original job?

66  Unfortunately there will be occasions when there is no reasonable adjustment or control measure that will enable an employee to return to their original job. Examples include the employee's failure to pass a statutory medical or the extent of the employee's physical limitations, or allergic conditions like occupational asthma or dermatitis caused by exposure to substances during work activities. You may find it difficult to identify these conditions, so consider seeking professional advice. One solution, other than for very small businesses, may be to offer the employee an alternative job and any necessary retraining. Sometimes continued employment is not feasible, but it is important not to jump to conclusions before you have explored alternative solutions.

67  The key issues for you and your employee regarding alternative work include checking that the alternative is suitable, the impact on their contractual terms and conditions including pay, any training or other support needed, and what the employee will do while alternatives are pursued.

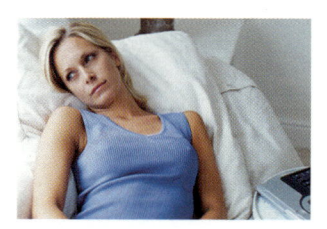

### Employment rights

68  The Employment Act 2002 (NI Employment Rights Order 2002) contains provisions for statutory minimum dismissal, disciplinary and grievance procedures. These are due to come into force in October 2004. For further advice on this and other employment legislation see Appendix 1, items 7 or 8 of Appendix 5 and the Department of Trade and Industry publications in Appendix 6.

69  Employment Tribunals recognise that employers, particularly small firms, cannot keep jobs open indefinitely or invent jobs that are not needed. They do expect you to make any reasonable adjustments to the job or working arrangements to enable a disabled employee to stay in their job. If this is not possible and there is alternative work that the employee would be capable of doing, the tribunal would normally expect you to offer it to the employee. See item 9 of Appendix 5 on how to contact the Employment Tribunal Service.

# Making use of professional or other advice and treatment

## When might professional or other advice be needed?

70  In many cases a straightforward adjustment such as gradual return to full-time working over a period of time will be enough to enable an ill, injured or disabled employee to return to work. But there will be circumstances where you or your employee will need professional or other specialist advice, and access to support or treatment before a return to work is possible. This section suggests ways of getting help with advice and treatment and should be read alongside the sections on planning adjustments and preparing a return to work plan. Appendix 5 provides contact details for a range of organisations and websites that can help employers and employees with health or disability matters. Useful publications are listed in Appendix 6. Sources of advice include:

- rehabilitation services providers, occupational health advisers, case managers, specialists in rehabilitation medicine (see items 55-66 of Appendix 5).
- HSE's Employment Medical Advisory Service (see items 14-15 of Appendix 5);
- Department for Work and Pensions Medical Services, particularly for SSP purposes (see item 10 of Appendix 5);
- Jobcentre Plus services (see items 12-13 of Appendix 5);
- case managers (see paragraph 96 and item 58 of Appendix 5);
- disability charities (see items 26-44);
- private medical, permanent health/income protection, and other insurers (see items 45-47 of Appendix 5);
- trade unions (see items 51-54 of Appendix 5);
- trade associations and other employer organisations (see items 48-50 of Appendix 5);
- the employee's GP (see Appendix 2).

71  NHS Direct (England and Wales) and NHS 24 (Scotland) are 24-hour advice services, staffed by nurses, which provide confidential information by telephone to your employees and their families on what to do if they feel ill (see items 21 and 22 of Appendix 5).

## Using professional advice from occupational health and rehabilitation services, insurers and others

72  If you employ occupational health practitioners or have a contract with independent providers of occupational health and rehabilitation services, you will be aware of the major role they can play in evaluating reasons for absence, carrying out health assessments, assisting you or your managers to plan an employee's return to work and talking to any other professionals and advisers involved. Even so, there may be situations when an employee still needs to be referred to a consultant or external service provider for specialist advice for employees with, eg major joint or muscle, heart or lung problems or therapy from a psychologist.

73  If yours is a small or medium enterprise, you may not have routine access to occupational health support though there are other sources of help like NHS Plus* (England only) and the disability employment services (Disability Advisory Service in NI) (see paragraphs 78-81). It might be possible for you to join together with other local businesses to fund contract services. Large employers could consider being a good neighbour by making their services available in some way to companies in their supply chain, or small local businesses.

* Some NHS Trusts in England only are able to sell occupational health support services to small and medium enterprises through NHS Plus, a network of NHS Occupational Health Departments which provide services to non-NHS employers. To join the network, OH units agreed to work to NHS quality standards. In addition, the NHS Plus website provides information and support to employees and employers alike and allows the user to identify their local provider.

74  Many insurers offer rehabilitation as part of their employers' liability insurance policies (see Appendix 3). Even where this is not the case, you should contact your insurer to find out about the use of rehabilitation as a means to reduce the impact of any injury.

75  Whether you employ or buy in occupational health or rehabilitation services, do bear in mind that the physicians, nurses and other professionals involved are bound by the obligations of their professions to provide independent and objective advice to both you and your employee. Unless they are seen to be impartial, employees will not trust any return to work advice the services provide. All health practitioners, whether or not they are employed by or

contracted to you also have a duty of confidence which prevents them from disclosing to an employer confidential personal information without the informed consent of the individual employee concerned (see paragraph 22 in Appendix 1). But note that even where consent has been refused, the occupational health adviser still has a duty to the employee to inform their employer about fitness for work issues where the employee's health and safety may be at risk.

## Helping with prompt provision of treatment

76  The longer an employee is off work the more challenging it becomes to manage their health problems. Long-term absence is also costly to you as an employer. It may be to your mutual benefit if you can help your employee to avoid long waiting times for, eg physiotherapy, medical treatment, counselling or psychological therapy, depending on the condition. Some organisations take this route, if the NHS is unable to deliver treatment in the shorter term and there is a reasonable hope of the employee returning to work. Help can be provided in a number of ways:

- one off payments or loans for private sector consultations or treatment;
- provision of private medical insurance for employees on a discounted or non-contributory basis;
- provision of permanent health, or income protection insurance under which the insurer assesses the employee's needs and helps them to get treatment;
- choosing wider coverage for employer's liability insurance that offers services to help claimants with work-related ill health to return to work (see also Appendix 3);
- employing or contracting with employee assistance programme providers to make counselling services available to employees.

## Taxable benefits

77  Payments, private medical insurance and income protection insurance may each be taxable to the employee. Services for work-related ill health and general welfare counselling are normally exempt from tax. Further information is given in HSE's free leaflet *Tax rules and the purchase of occupational health support* (see Appendix 6).

### Case study
An electrical company has set up rehabilitation programmes for employees in their power distribution business with muscle, bone and joint disorders.
- A forty-year-old linesman suffered a cervical disc lesion resulting in weakness and muscle wasting in his left arm. He was absent from work for four months but after a two week programme which included graduated exercise, hydrotherapy and gym work, he had improved his muscle strength and was able to return to his normal duties.
- A long-standing back problem kept a fifty-five year old mechanical fitter off work regularly. During the latest absence, he suffered constant pain, restricted mobility and depression. But, after a three week course of exercises, physiotherapy, hydrotherapy, gym work and pain management, the future looked much brighter, as he was able to return to work on a phased plan.

## How can I get help with reasonable adjustments for disabled employees?

78  If you or your employee needs assistance with reasonable adjustments, your employee can apply to the nearest Jobcentre Plus (in NI, Jobs and Benefits office) for help. A Disability Employment Adviser will advise whether the Access to Work (AtW) Scheme can help and refer you and your employee to an AtW Adviser. The types of support and advice the scheme provides covers, eg:

- adaptations to a vehicle, or help towards taxi fares or other transport costs if public transport is not accessible;
- alterations to premises to provide better access;
- new equipment or adaptations to existing equipment;
- support workers eg services of a reader at work for blind or visually impaired employees, or for people who need practical help at work or getting to work.

79  The AtW Adviser will normally speak to you and your employee to find the most effective solution. In the majority of cases, this can be done over the telephone, but a visit can be arranged if necessary. Sometimes specialist or technical advice may be needed, which the AtW Adviser will help arrange. You are responsible for buying any equipment needed or carrying out alterations, but subject to an assessment, you may be able to claim a grant for doing so from AtW.

80  Disability Employment Advisers (DEAs) based at Jobcentre Plus offices (in NI, Jobs and Benefits office) can also provide you with support and advice in adopting good employment practice in recruiting, retaining, training and career development of disabled people.

81  If you or your employee have concerns about the effects of their disability on work, the DEA can give both of you practical advice on job redesign, adjustments at work, and avoiding job loss. If the employee has been off work for some time the DEA can provide an employment assessment to help them find out how their disability or health condition will affect their work and the action necessary to help them return. The DEA may recommend referral of the employee to a work preparation programme individually designed to help the employee regain confidence. In cases where return to existing duties is not possible, the DEA may be able to give advice about the employee's capability to develop new skills.

### Case study

When a street lighting coordinator had his leg amputated due to a long-term medical condition, his employers were quick to consider how to assist him to return to work.

An AtW application was completed and an AtW adviser made recommendations regarding ramps, access to the building and workstation and referred the employee to a physiotherapist. He attended an assessment at the regional Disability Services to try chairs, leg rests and desks, a suitable chair was chosen and made available.

As the existing desk height was too low, an adjustment was made by raising the desk with 5 cm blocks to provide adequate legroom. He was allocated a company car with automatic transmission to enable him to fulfil driving duties. His working hours and duties were modified to allow a structured return to work three months after his operation.

Making use of professional or other advice and treatment

## What if my employee's ill health is caused by conflicts at work?

82   Conflicts can normally be avoided if everyone in the workplace understands and agrees the standard of acceptable behaviour expected from them (see also paragraph 38). But sometimes people do not realise that their behaviour causes distress or unexpected circumstances occur which cause conflict. One way of tackling this is to use the services of qualified workplace mediators, many of whom will be members of other professions such as human resources, counselling, coaching and consultancy. Such mediators can be found by using local directories, human resource journals or through the World Wide Web by entering key words such as 'workplace mediation' or 'conflict resolution'. Case managers (see paragraph 96) can also act as mediators.

### Case study

Two managers found themselves chasing the same commission as a result of winning a piece of business. Each felt that the other had stolen his right to the money and they started to argue, stopped co-operating and made abusive remarks in front of others. The atmosphere soon became stressful, for themselves and others. One became ill and took sick leave, the other asked for a transfer, both submitted formal complaints about the other's behaviour.

The employees were given the option of a facilitated meeting to explore their differences in private with the help of professional workplace mediators. The employees were cautious at first, but soon found that they shared an interest in ensuring that the company's bonus system did not put colleagues in a similar situation again.

In just one day, two mediators helped them to begin talking again and they resolved to work together to change the process. Both complaints were withdrawn, saving the company £23 000 in procedural costs and restoring the employees' sense of dignity and control over their situation.

Similar processes can be used when, eg relations between an employee and their line manager have broken down.

# Agreeing and reviewing a return to work plan

## Agreeing a return to work plan

83   Once you have identified adjustments, and have all the advice you need about what your employee can and cannot do, whether temporarily or permanently, the next step is to prepare a return to work plan. To help the plan succeed you need to consult everyone affected by it, but particularly the employee concerned. Empowering the individual to influence their own return to work is an important element of increasing their well-being and confidence.

84   A plan may also be useful to agree alternative working arrangements for employees who have not been absent but are in poorer health (eg undergoing treatment) or to keep working in circumstances such as a partner's serious illness.

## When is the right time to prepare a plan?

85   Beginning to develop the plan at an appropriate time is crucial. Discussing a plan too soon may put employees under pressure, particularly when there are underlying work issues that need to be tackled, such as workload pressures or bullying and harassment. But leaving it too late may mean the employee loses confidence in their ability to return even with appropriate support. The right time will depend on the person concerned and the nature of their illness, injury or disability.

86   In many cases the best time to prepare a plan is three-four weeks into the absence. Normally people will return to work under their own steam in the weeks before. In the case of injury or post-operative convalescence, there may be clear physical milestones in the healing process that will influence the plan. If you are in the catering or food manufacturing industries, the plan may be influenced by your duties under the Food Safety Act 1990 and related regulations to protect the public from food safety risks (see paragraph 24 in Appendix 1).

87   In the case of depression or other mental ill health, it may mean a step-by-step process. You may need to consider seeking professional advice to establish when they are ready to plan and when they can actually return. The absent employee may need help to achieve simple life goals like getting up at a certain time, and going to the corner shop, before thinking about return to work.

## Who should put the plan together?

88   This will depend upon the circumstances. In many cases involving planned adjustments, or a gradual return to work, you or the employee's line manager will be able to prepare the plan together with the employee, trade union or other employee representatives and other employees affected. Disability charities and Jobcentre Plus (in NI, Jobs and Benefit office) services are able to offer advice. When input is needed from a number of advisers the plan may need to be drawn up by the person co-ordinating the employee's return (see paragraphs 93-96). In the case of serious injury or mental illness, occupational health advisers, the employee's GP, hospital consultants or specialists such as psychiatrists may also need to be involved.

## What needs to go into the plan?

89   The plan needs to be tailored to the specific needs of the employee concerned. It can take the form of a simple chart or table (useful in the case of a gradual return to full-time work) or a written statement, whatever is most suitable to the circumstances. The content needs to:

- take account of any advice you or your employee have received from their GP, your occupational health adviser, disability employment advisory services etc;
- reflect the needs of your employee and your organisation.

90   It is useful to include:

- the approximate date of the employee's return to work;
- the goal of the return to work, eg return to a modified work role or system, or alternative working hours, whether on a temporary or permanent basis;
- the time period of the plan;
- a statement of alternative working arrangements;
- information about any impact on terms and conditions;
- what checks will be made to make sure it is put into practice;
- dates when the plan will be reviewed with the employee, and by whom;
- signatures of agreement – employee, line manager etc.

## Putting the plan into operation

91  Before you put the plan into operation, check that:

- the plan does not require the employee to return before they are ready;
- the employee understands the impact on their pay;
- the plan takes into account:
    - the views and advice of the employee concerned;
    - any professional or specialist advice provided to the employee by their GP, occupational health adviser, or disability advisers;
    - any views and advice of the trade union and other employee representatives;
- control measures have been put in place (see paragraph 62) if alternative arrangements could affect the health and safety of the employees' teammates, eg through extra workload;
- obligations, under the DDA, to provide reasonable adjustments are met and regularly reviewed;
- the plan has the support and agreement of the employee and their supervisor, other managers as appropriate, and the teammates affected;
- steps have been taken to keep everyone informed and make sure the plan is respected;
- arrangements have been made to review the plan with the employee and trade union or other employee representatives at suitable intervals and at its end;
- everyone affected is clear about their responsibilities, including who will review the plan.

92  It is essential that the plan is understood, implemented properly and kept under close review. Make sure that everyone knows where they stand and that employees and managers are not subject to conflicting demands from, eg production targets and the employee's need for reduced hours. If the employee cannot cope, they may become disheartened, take more sick leave and end up out of pocket. End of plan reviews will help you and your employee decide if the plan needs to be extended and changed. Look out for lessons that could apply to future plans involving other employees.

# Co-ordinating the return to work process

## When might a co-ordinator be necessary?

93   If you have had to get assistance from a number of advisers inside and outside the workplace it may be helpful to appoint someone to act as a go-between or co-ordinator. The co-ordinator's role would be to make sure that information is available in time, arrangements proceed smoothly and everyone concerned knows and understands what to expect. The type of person who should take this on will vary according to the circumstances.

94   If yours is a reasonably small business, you or the employee's supervisor may be able to act as the co-ordinator in a fairly informal way, perhaps with external advice. In some cases, a trade union or other employee representative may be able to act as co-ordinator. In large organisations, other possible personnel include a line manager, human resources, equal opportunities or occupational health professional.

95   Whoever is chosen, it is important that they are familiar with the employee's work environment and job content, able to communicate and negotiate with staff at all levels, and sensitive to the needs of the employee concerned, including any disability issues. Information about employee's health should not be shared without that employee's informed consent (see paragraphs 52 and 75 in the main text, and paragraph 22 in Appendix 1 and 4 in Appendix 2).

## Using a case manager

96   A more formal approach to co-ordination, known as 'case management' may be needed in complicated cases or when input from a number of specialists (eg occupational health practitioners, specialists in rehabilitation medicine, physiotherapists, psychologists and disability advisers), in addition to human resource staff, health and safety professionals, trade union and other employee representatives and GPs is necessary. Case managers can also mediate in cases where communications have broken down or help is needed to move things on. A 'case manager' is typically someone who is professionally qualified in a relevant medical area and may be involved in the treatment of the returning employee. The case management approach is widely used in Australia to help ill and injured employees back to work and is beginning to be recognised in Britain. The Case Management Society of the UK can provide more information (see item 58 in Appendix 5). Alternatively, if an insurance company is involved, they may be willing to perform this function.

**Case study**

An employee, working as a delivery driver, was assaulted by members of the public, which resulted in stabbing wounds to his back. The driver's employer notified their insurer, who also provided rehabilitation services, early in the case. Two days after the incident, a medical case manager from the insurer arranged counselling, which began within a week. In addition, the employee's GP recommended physiotherapy to treat complications resulting from the physical injury.

The employee returned to work on light duties as recommended, within two months. The employer commented that they were impressed with his conduct throughout the recovery period and would keep him in mind for management positions.

Four months after the incident, the employee began full duties in the same area where the assault took place. The medical case manager has continued to liaise with the employer and employee throughout the process.

# Developing a policy on return to work and putting it into practice

## Do I need to develop a policy?

97 If your business is very small, helping an employee to return after longer term sick leave or to stay in post following illness or disability may be a 'one-off' event. All you may need to do is to think through in advance, with the help of your workforce, including any trade union and other employee representatives:

- how you would manage the situation;
- what reasonable adjustments you could make.

98 The more employees you have, the more likely it is that you will have to manage a number of them who are in poorer health. It is important that your overall approach is fair, consistent and disability-aware even though you may need to be flexible on the detail of an individual employee's return to work plan. Your employees need to know what to expect, managers need to understand their roles and everyone needs to be clear about who is responsible for action. Although you are not legally required to provide a return to work policy, it is often convenient to set expectations, roles and responsibilities down in a written return to work policy, so you have something to refer to.

## How do I go about preparing a policy statement?

99 **Advice on the content of a written policy is given in Appendix 4 to this guidance.** As with any other company or organisational policy, it will only work if it has active support from you, your employees and, if you have them, your senior managers, health and safety, occupational and human resource professionals, line managers, trade union and other employee representatives. If you are a manager rather than the employer, you will need to secure your employers'/senior managers' support for developing a policy. A good way to begin is by talking to your managers, and workers, including trade union and other employee representatives, and employees with experience of longer term absence about their needs and expectations of a return to work policy.

100 You may have a very good return to work policy in writing, but there is no guarantee that it will be effective in practice unless all your employees:

- know, understand and fully support its content;
- are confident that it is properly put into operation whenever an ill, injured or disabled employee needs help to return to work and/or stay in post.

101 Employees who have become ill, injured or disabled are likely to be very anxious about the future and suspicious of your intentions. They may see a request that they have an assessment or talk to an occupational health specialist as the first step towards dismissal or compulsory retirement. They will need reassurance that the policy is about safeguarding employees' health, helping them to stay in work and improving the business, not job loss. An open style of management, and discussion, in which trade union and other employee representatives take part and contribute feedback on the way it is working, will encourage trust and ownership of the policy.

102 Employee confidence will also be boosted if they can see that you and your senior management are interested in and actively committed to encouraging return to work and not just paying lip service to the policy.

## Helping your line managers and supervisors to support the policy

103 Line managers and supervisors have an important part to play in preventing poor health from becoming worse and managing an employee's return to work after absence. They are often best placed to spot signs of stress, or poor movement due to muscle or joint pain, among employees. But they may need help with understanding where their responsibilities lie, and taking action in a confident but sensitive way.

104 Managers or supervisors need to know and understand:

- their responsibilities for managing the attendance and return to work of ill, injured or disabled employees;
- what company or organisational funds might be available for workplace adjustments;
- what unified help and support they can expect within the company or organisation, eg from occupational health, personnel, diversity and health and safety managers;
- they too are employees who can expect help to return to work if they become ill, injured or disabled.

Consider whether they need training in any of the following:

- managing staff to promote good working relationships;
- working with trade union and other employee representatives;

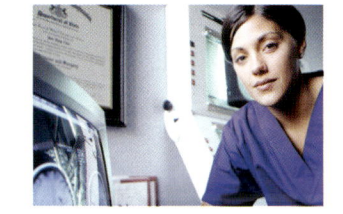

- putting the company policy on return to work into practice;
- communication skills in keeping up contact with absent employees;
- DDA awareness;
- introducing workplace adjustments;
- stress awareness.

### Welcoming returning employees back

105  Do take account of the attitudes of a returning employee's fellow workers as these could make or break a successful return. Teammates may not be ready to welcome back someone they see as not pulling their weight, likely to reduce team bonuses, or receiving more favourable treatment, eg through shorter hours. You can promote more positive attitudes and trust by encouraging open discussion. Working with employees and their trade union and other representatives will help you to find flexible solutions, whether temporary or permanent, which do not disadvantage anyone (see the first case study on page 13).

106  The first day back at work after sickness absence of several weeks or months can be a big hurdle for the returning employee. As well as a return to work interview, they will need someone to welcome them back, ensure their workspace is ready for them and bring them up to speed with changes. An informal visit to the workplace can break the ice before the employee actually returns to work.

### Promoting awareness and understanding of disability and ill health

107  Fellow workers are more likely to accept different arrangements if they understand the nature of returning employees' health problems in general terms. Many people may lack knowledge or draw wrong conclusions about health conditions or disabilities and their effect on capability to work. This can often be the case with mental health conditions, although most people who experience ongoing mental health problems can continue to work effectively with little or no support. One way of overcoming negative attitudes, often caused by fear or embarrassment, is by providing training in awareness of particular health conditions for everyone. But it is also important that employees who have experienced mental illness are treated in the same way as those with physical ill health.

**And finally**.........There is much that you can do to make sure that you do not lose valuable employees through sickness and that they can continue in fulfilling employment. Taking action to keep employees in work saves on recruitment and training costs, improves your organisation's reputation and could give you a competitive edge in today's economy.

# Appendix 1 Relevant Legislation

This Appendix describes some legal requirements that are relevant to the return to work and retention of ill, injured and disabled employees. It is not a definitive guide to the Acts and Regulations listed. The abbreviation NI stands for Northern Ireland legislation.

**Health and Safety at Work etc Act 1974 (HSWA)/Northern Ireland Health and Safety at Work etc Order 1978 (HSWO)**

1  This legislation places duties on everyone concerned with work activities, including employers, self-employed people, employees, manufacturers and designers. The duties are imposed both on individual people and on corporations, companies, partnerships, local authorities etc. They apply to all types of work activities and situations.

2  Section 2 of HSWA and article 4 of HSWO require all employers to ensure, so far as is reasonably practicable, the health, safety and welfare at work of all their employees. The most important areas relate to:

- the provision and maintenance of plant (eg machinery and equipment), and systems of work, so that they are safe without risks to health;
- the use, handling, storage and transport of articles and substances at work;
- the provision of information, instruction, training and supervision, as necessary;
- the provision and maintenance of a working environment that is safe and free of risks to health;
- where there are five or more employees, the provision of a written statement of their general policy on the health and safety at work of employees.

3  In the case of employees who are returning to work after sick leave, or who have ongoing poorer health, employers need to:

- make sure that those employees' health is not made worse by work; and
- take steps to prevent or control risks to which those employees may be exposed due to the lasting symptoms or effects of an injury, illness or disability.

## Management of Health and Safety at Work Regulations (MHSWR) 1999 (NI MHSWR 2000)

4   These regulations set out broad general duties that apply to almost all kinds of work. They place a number of requirements on employers that include:

- making a suitable and sufficient assessment of the risks to the health and safety of employees in the workplace that could harm the health and safety of their employees and others who may be affected by the work activities;
- introducing preventive and protective measures to control risks identified by the risk assessment;
- reviewing and if necessary modifying that assessment and the preventive and protective measures if circumstances change, eg if work could affect the health of an employee returning following sick leave or an employee's health affects the way they perform tasks at work;
- providing employees with a level of health surveillance (ie watching over their health by various methods) that is appropriate to any risks to their health and safety that are identified by the risk assessment.

*Risk assessment*

5   The purpose of a risk assessment is to examine what could cause harm in the workplace and consider how likely it is that people could be harmed by the things examined. Employers then need to decide whether they have taken enough precautions to prevent people being harmed or that more control measures are needed.

6   If the employee's illness, injury or disability is work related, steps must be taken to prevent or control risks that could lead to more cases of injury, illness or disability or the worsening of existing ones.

7   When assessing risks, deciding on preventive and protective measures, and putting adjustments in place, employers must consult their company's or organisation's trade union safety representative(s) or an elected representative of employee safety (see paragraphs 10-13 of this Appendix).

8   Other relevant duties which the MHSWR place on employers include:
- appointing competent people to help devise and apply the measures needed to comply with employer's duties under health and safety law;
- giving employees information about health and safety matters;
- providing information for people working in their undertaking who are not their employees;
- making sure employees have adequate health and safety training and are capable enough at their jobs to avoid risk.

## Health and Safety (Miscellaneous Amendments) Regulations 2002 (NI 2003) that amended the Workplace (Health, Safety and Welfare) Regulations 1992 (NI 1993)

9   There were two amendments to the Workplace Regulations made in 2002 that address the needs of disabled workers within the workplace, by requiring employers to ensure that:

- doors, passageways, stairs, lavatories and workstations are suitably arranged to take account of their needs; and
- rest facilities cater for disabled people's needs.

## Safety Representatives and Safety Committees Regulations 1977 (NI 1977)

10   These regulations set out the role of trade union appointed safety representatives, which is to work alongside employers to reduce health and safety risks within the workplace.

11   Safety representatives' rights and functions include a legal right to represent employees in discussions with the employer on health, safety or welfare issues and in discussions with HSE, HSENI, or other enforcing authorities.

12   A safety representative has no legal duties, other than those of an employee. Employers must consult trade union safety representatives on all matters relating to employee health and safety.

## The Health and Safety (Consultation with Employees) Regulations 1996 (NI 1996)

13   These Regulations provide that any employees not in groups covered by trade union appointed safety representatives must be consulted on health and safety matters by their employers. The employer can choose to consult them directly or through elected representatives of employee safety.

## Disability Discrimination Act 1995

14 The Disability Discrimination Act (DDA) 1995 aims to promote the employment and welfare of disabled people by requiring employers to ensure that their employment practices are not discriminatory. From October 2004, the Act will apply to all employers whatever the number of people they employ. It covers all aspects of employment from recruitment and selection, through terms and conditions, training and career development, to retention and dismissal. Employers are required to make reasonable adjustments to the workplace or employment arrangements, so that a disabled person is not at any substantial disadvantage compared to a non-disabled person (see also paragraphs 44-49 and 58 of the main text).

15 The Act defines a person as disabled if they have a physical or mental impairment that has a substantial (ie not minor or trivial) and long-term adverse effect on their ability to carry out normal day-to-day activities.

16 As well as conditions that affect the senses, (eg blindness or deafness), or the the loss of mobility or dexterity, *impairments* include mental illness, learning disabilities, dyslexia, diabetes and facial disfigurement.

17 *Long term* means it has lasted for, or is likely to last more than twelve months, or the rest of the disabled person's life. This includes conditions like epilepsy or asthma or degenerative diseases.

18 *Normal day-to-day activities are defined as:*

- mobility;
- physical coordination;
- continence;
- perception of the risk of physical danger;
- manual dexterity;
- ability to lift, carry or move everyday objects;
- speaking, hearing or seeing;
- memory or ability to concentrate, learn or understand.

19 Harassment on account of disability will be expressly outlawed from October 2004. An employer can be deemed responsible for acts of harassment carried out by staff unless he can show he took reasonable steps to prevent it – like making it clear that it is a serious disciplinary matter.

## Employment Rights Act 1996 (NI Employment Rights Order 1996)

20 Under this Act, employers must adopt a fair procedure, subject to certain conditions, before deciding to dismiss an employee for sickness absence.

## Employment Act 2002 (NI Employment Rights Order 2003)

21 The Act puts in place statutory minimum dismissal, disciplinary, and grievance procedures. Regulations that will implement these are due to come into force in October 2004.

## The Access to Medical Reports Act 1988 (The Access to Personal Files and Medical Reports (NI) Order 1991)

22 This legislation allows people a right of access to any medical reports on them supplied by a medical practitioner for employment or insurance purposes. It also prevents the disclosure of a medical report to anybody other than the person named in the report unless they have consented to its release. If consent is given then the person concerned has the right to see the report before it is released and 21 days are allowed for this to happen. The medical practitioner is required to keep any report they release for six months.

## Data Protection Act 1998

23 The Act makes provision for the regulation of the processing of information relating to individuals, including the obtaining, holding, use or disclosure of such information. Further information on how employers can process sickness and accident records can be found in Part 2 of the Employment Practices Protection Code and for medical records in draft Part 4 of the Code.

## Food Safety (General Food Hygiene) Regulations 1995 (NI 1995)

24 These Regulations set out the basic hygiene requirements that food businesses must follow in relation to staff, premises and food handling, including a duty on food business proprietors not to permit people with certain medical conditions to work in a food handling area.

# Appendix 2  GP advice on returning to work

1   The Department for Work and Pensions (DWP) issues official guidance, based upon law, to all registered medical practitioners in England, Scotland and Wales (see also item 10 of Appendix 5). Similar guidance applies in Northern Ireland. GPs have a statutory obligation to provide their patients with advice on fitness for work and to record this advice on official statements, such as the Form Med 3 certificate.*

*Medical certificates seen by employers:

Med 3: Following seven calendar days of absence your employee must get a medical certificate, Med 3, from their GP to cover their period of sickness. The GP must see your employee on the day of issuing the Med 3 or the previous day.

Med 5: This medical certificate is used to supply evidence of your employee's incapacity for work from earlier periods not covered by a Med 3. The GP signing the medical certificate must have examined the patient on a previous occasion and be sure they would have advised your employee to refrain from work from the date of that earlier examination for the entire period of the medical certificate or based their advice on a report from another GP issued less than one month previously. In the latter case the GP will issue a Med 5 to cover a forward period of no more than one month.

2   The DWP guidance advises doctors that they should always consider carefully whether advising a patient to refrain from work is the most appropriate clinical management and that doctors may often best help a patient of working age by taking action that will encourage and support job retention and rehabilitation. The guidance also encourages GPs to consider work adjustments as an alternative to signing patients off work and provides information on evidence-based recovery times for a small number of common operations, to help them decide how long a patient should remain off work.

3   GPs may use the Med 3 sick note:

- to advise a patient who has recovered that they are fit to return to work; or
- where appropriate to advise a patient that their condition need not require them to refrain from work – in which case the GP may suggest possible work restrictions and adjustments.

As employees can self certify for the first seven days of a spell of sickness absence, GPs are not obliged to provide sick notes, such as Med 3, to cover this period and employers cannot insist on their provision.

## Can I contact my sick employee's GP?

4   GPs are there to provide care and treatment for their patients. They have no duties to provide employers with information and they cannot legally do so without that patient's full understanding and agreement. If consent is given, GPs are able to provide you with general advice on the patient's capacity on a need-to-know basis but they are not under any contractual obligation to do so. Most GPs will not have the expertise to advise on detailed workplace modifications.

5   When writing to a GP to request information on an employee's likelihood of a return to work and when that may be, it is helpful to include:

- what the company or organisation does;
- the employee's tasks or duties or a job description (including any materials or substances used and specific requirements such as working at heights or use of respiratory or other protective equipment);
- where they work and with whom they work;
- hours of work, shift patterns and any relevant overtime arrangements;
- the company or organisational policy on return to work;
- what adjustments could be offered.

Remember to give a copy of your letter to the employee concerned. GPs are entitled to request a reasonable professional fee for a medical report for providing factual information.

# Appendix 3 Employers' liability insurance (ELCI/ELDECI)

1   The Employers' Liability (Compulsory Insurance) Act 1969 (ELCI) and the Employers Liability (Defective Equipment and Compulsory Insurance) (Northern Ireland) Order 1972 (ELDECI) require most employers to insure against liability for injury or disease to their employees arising out of their employment. ELCI and ELDECI ensure employers have a minimum level of insurance cover against claims from employees and former employees for such compensation.

2   In many cases involving damages for personal injuries, the claimant's expectations of recovery and long-term quality of life would be improved by prompt treatment (eg within four to six weeks) and provision of any necessary aids. Unfortunately, consideration of blame in such cases can cause delay to treatment and provision of aids for the claimant.

3   The insurance industry has recognised that more can be achieved for the claimant by providing treatment and other help to stay in employment than through compensation alone. Some insurers offer wider cover for ELCI and ELDECI that includes services to help the claimant recover, and where possible get back to work. The International Underwriting Association and the Association of British Insurers Rehabilitation Working Party has issued a revised code of best practice, *The Rehabilitation Code* (see Appendix 6). The code has the support of the Association of Personal Injury Lawyers, the Forum of Injury Lawyers, the Bodily Injury Claims Management Association (BICMA), the Association of British Insurers and the International Underwriting Association.

The aim of the code is to ensure that:

- the claimant's solicitor and the insurer actively consider the use of rehabilitation services and the benefits of an early assessment of the claimant's needs; and
- the claimant's long-term physical and mental well-being is treated as being equally as important as the payment of proper compensation.

It is available from BICMA (see Appendix 6).

# Appendix 4 Suggested content of a return to work policy

1   There is no legal requirement to provide a policy statement on return to work. This Appendix offers suggestions directly to you as an employer.

## What should a written policy look like?

2   There is no one size fits all, the format needs to be one that suits your circumstances. It could consist of a statement or a set of guidelines, ranging from half a page of short points for a small company to a longer, more detailed document for large companies with expert resources. It is useful to:

- consider whether the written policy should stand alone or form part of other company or organisational policy documents, eg equal opportunities guidelines or staff handbooks;
- make sure the messages and information given by linked documents are consistent with one another;
- draw a clear distinction between information on disciplinary procedures and guidance for helping employees back to work;
- avoid confusion by not including the policy in statements that you are *legally* required to provide, eg the health and safety policy statement, which you must provide under the HSWA.

## What do I need to include in a written policy?

3   Information that is useful to put into a policy statement includes:

- your or your organisation's commitment to helping employees return to work;
- confirmation that your employees can expect you will:
  - work with trade union representatives and other employee representatives on developing and reviewing the operation of the return to work policy;
  - make reasonable adjustments to retain an employee who has become disabled or whose disability has worsened, so that they are not put at a substantial disadvantage in their job;
  - support returns to work, eg in the form of adjustments to the workplace or changes to systems or hours of work wherever possible and redeployment where this is necessary;
  - agree return to work plans with everyone affected;
  - ensure that employees who have suffered ill health, injury or disability will be treated fairly, equally and consistently;
- your arrangements for recording sickness absence, as appropriate;
- provision of leave and time off to aid return to work or to attend medical appointments;
- procedures for keeping in contact with staff on sick leave and what is expected from the employee;
- arrangements for return to work interviews;
- how the policy links in with other key policies, such as personnel, health and safety, equal opportunities etc and company employee benefit schemes.

4   If your organisation has a line management structure and access to human resource or occupational health support, you may also wish to consider including:

- what action line managers should take and when and how the action will be supported (see paragraphs 103-104 of the main text);
- responsibilities for putting the return to work plan into action and reviewing its progress;
- sources of advice within the organisation on what can be done to help an employee's return to work and continued employment;
- help that can be given to employees by government agencies, charitable bodies and other industry and specialist organisations;
- the information that needs to be provided and requested when making occupational health or other medical referrals.

5   Mental and physical ill health caused by stress, whether from pressures at or away from the workplace is one of the main reasons employees take sick leave. When larger companies develop return to work policies, some find it helpful to either devote part of their statement to stress-related illness or make it the subject of a separate statement. Take care with this approach, so as not to make people with stress-related conditions feel isolated or different in any way. But if stress-related illness is a particular problem in your organisation, perhaps because of the nature of its work, it may be helpful to set out:

- a commitment to increasing awareness and understanding of stress-related conditions;
- steps that managers should take to identify and prevent cases of excessive pressure or other types of demand being placed on people, including:
  - making adjustments and return to work plans;
  - how advice will be provided to help employees cope with stress;

Appendix 4 Suggested content of a return to work policy

- advice on dealing with, and preventing, harassment and bullying;
- a commitment to using HSE's guidance on stress management.

## Key actions for a successful policy statement

- Discuss and agree the content with trade union representatives.
- Get the practice right – consider piloting it before committing it to a statement.
- Write the content in plain language, making sure it is clear who is responsible and accountable for carrying out any actions or procedures.
- Make sure everyone understands their responsibilities and has the skills and knowledge to put them into practice and provide training if necessary.
- Check that procedures are put into operation and they are carried out consistently for all employees affected.
- Invite feedback from employees and from trade union and other employee representatives and review the content regularly.
- Keep factual information up to date.

# Appendix 5  Organisations that can provide further advice

This is not a definitive list but provides a useful cross section of organisations that can provide relevant advice.

## Government Departments, statutory bodies, etc

*Data protection*
1. Information Commissioner's Office
   Wycliffe House, Water Lane, Wilmslow,
   Cheshire SK9 5AF
   Data Protection Helpline: 01625 545 745
   Website: www.informationcommissioner.gov.uk
   e-mail: mail@ico.gsi.gov.uk

*Disability information*
2. Department for Work and Pensions
   Disability Unit, Level 6, Adelphi building,
   John Adams Street, London WC2N 6HT
   Website: www.disability.gov.uk
   e-mail: enquiry-disability@dwp.gsi.gov.uk

3. (Northern Ireland) Department for
   Employment and Learning (DEL)
   Adelaide House, 39/49 Adelaide Street,
   Belfast BT2 8FD
   Tel: 028 9025 7777
   Website: www.delni.gov.uk

4. Disability Rights Commission (DRC)
   Freepost MID02164, Stratford-upon-Avon CV37 9BR
   DRC Helpline: 08457 622 633
   Textphone: 08457 622 644
   Website: www.drc-gb.org

*Employment Relations (see also Trade union advice)*
5. Advisory Conciliation and Arbitration Service (ACAS)
   Helpline: 08457 47 47 47
   Website: www.acas.org.uk
   (see the website for your regional office)

6. (Northern Ireland) Labour Relations Agency
   2–8 Gordon Street, Belfast BT1 2LG
   Tel: 028 9032 1442
   Website: www.lra.org.uk

7. Department for Trade and Industry
   Public Enquiry Unit, 1 Victoria Street,
   London SW1H 0ET
   Tel: 020 7215 5000
   Website: www.dti.gov.uk
   e-mail: dti.enquiries@dti.gsi.gov.uk

8. (Northern Ireland) Department for Trade,
   Enterprise and Investment
   Netherleigh Massey Avenue, Belfast BT4 2JP
   Tel: 028 9052 9900
   Website: www.detini.gov.uk

9. Employment Tribunal Service
   Website: www.ets.gov.uk (see the website for your local employment tribunal)

*Employment Services and State Benefits*
10. Department for Work and Pensions
    Correspondence Unit, Room 540, The Adelphi,
    1-11 John Adam Street, London WC2N 6HT
    Tel: 020 7712 2171
    Website: www.dwp.gov.uk (and
    www.dwp.gov.uk/medical for information about
    fitness for work advice provided by NHS GPs and
    statutory certification)

11. For benefits advice in Northern Ireland contact:
    Social Security Agency for Northern Ireland,
    Castle Court, Royal Avenue, Belfast BT1 1SD
    Benefit Enquiry Line: 0800 220 674
    Industrial Injuries Branch: 028 9033 6000

12. Jobcentre Plus
    Website: www.jobcentreplus.gov.uk
    (see the website for your local Jobcentre Plus office)

13. For Northern Ireland employment services,
    see DEL, item 3

*Health and safety*
14. The Health and Safety Executive (England, Scotland and Wales) (HSE)
    Website: www.hse.gov.uk (particularly
    www.hse.gov.uk/sicknessabsence, www.hse.gov.uk/stress
    and www. hse.gov.uk/msd)

- HSE Information Services,
  Caerphilly Business Park, Caerphilly CF83 3GG
  Infoline: 08701 545500
  e-mail: hseinformationservices@natbrit.com

Appendix 5  Organisations that can provide further advice

- HSE Books, PO Box 1999, Sudbury, Suffolk CO10 2WA
  Tel: 01787 881165

- HSE Employment Medical Advisory Service – look for details of your local HSE office in the telephone directory or on HSE's website

- In Scotland, see also item 19 below

15  **The Health and Safety Executive for Northern Ireland (HSENI)**
Website: www.hseni.gov.uk

- HSENI helpline: 0800 0320 121

- Employment Medical Advisory Service
  Tel: 028 9054 2122

*Health Information*

16  **The Department of Health (England only)**
(see also 21 and 23 below for NHS)
Customer Service Centre, Richmond House,
79 Whitehall, London SW1A 2NL
Tel: 020 7210 4850
Website: www.doh.gov.uk
e-mail: dohmail@dh.gsi.gov.uk (see also item 10)

17  **Welsh Assembly Government's Health and Social Care Department**
Cathays Park, Cardiff CF10 3NQ (see also item 21)
Tel: 029 20 825111
Website: www.wales.gov.uk
e-mail: www.health.enquiries@wales.gsi.gov.uk

18  **Scottish Executive Health Department**
(see also item 22)
St Andrews House, Regent Road, Edinburgh EH1 3DG
Tel: 0131 556 8400
Website: www.show.scot.nhs.uk/sehd/
e-mail: ceu@scotland.gov.uk

19  **Health Education Board for Scotland's Safe and Healthy Working Service for Small Businesses**
Adviceline: 0800 019 2211
Website: www.hebs.com/safeandhealthyworking

20  **(Northern Ireland) Department for Health, Social Services and Public Safety**
Castle Buildings, Stormont, Belfast BT4 3SJ
Tel: 028 905 20500
Website: www.dhsspsni.gov.uk

21  **NHS Direct:** (England and Wales)
*(Personal health advice)*
Website: www.nhsdirect.nhs.uk
Tel: 0845 46 47

22  **NHS 24** (Scotland only) *(Personal health advice)*
Tel: 08454 24 24 24
Website: www.nhs24.com

23  **NHS Plus** (England only) *(Occupational Health Services)*
Tel: 0800 092 0062
Website: www.nhsplus.nhs.uk
e-mail: nhsplus@doh.gsi.gov.uk

*Local Authorities*

24  See *Yellow Pages* for your local authority's Environmental Health Office. See also item 50 for LA employers' organisation

*Statutory Sick Pay*

25  Inland Revenue
Website: www.inlandrevenue.gov.uk (see the website for your local Inland Revenue enquiry centre and relevant enquiry helpline or for medical assessment advice, contact DWP medical services (see item 10)

## Charities

26  **Action for Blind People**
Action for Blind People, 14-16 Verney Road,
London SE16 3DZ
Tel: 020 7635 4800
Website: www.afbp.org
e-mail: info@afbp.org

27  **Association of Disabled Professionals**
BCM ADP, London WC1N 3XX
Tel: 020 8778 5008
Website: www.adp.org.uk
e-mail: adp.admin@ntlworld.com

28  **BackCare**
16 Elmtree Road, Teddington, Middlesex TW11 8ST
Tel: 020 8977 5474
Website: www.backcare.org.uk

29  **British Heart Foundation**
14 Fitzhardinge Street, London W1H 6DH
Tel: 020 7935 0185
Website: www.bhf.org.uk

Appendix 5 Organisations that can provide further advice

30 **Changing Faces** *(Advice on disfigurement)*
1 and 2 Junction Mews, London W2 1PN
Tel: 0845 4500 275
Website: www.changingfaces.co.uk
e-mail: info@changingfaces.co.uk

31 **The Employers' Forum on Disability**
Nutmeg House, 60 Gainsford Street, London SE1 2NY
Tel: 020 7403 3020
Website: www.employers-forum.co.uk
e-mail: website.enquiries@employers-forum.co.uk

32 **Employment Opportunities for People with Disabilities**
123 Minories, London EC3N 1NT
Tel: 020 7481 2727
Website: www.opportunities.org.uk
e-mail: info@eopps.org

33 **Guide Dogs for the Blind Association**
Hillfields, Burghfield Common, Reading RG7 3YG
Tel: 0870 600 2323
Website: www.guidedogs.org.uk
e-mail: guidedogs@guidedogs.org.uk

34 **Mind**
PO Box 277, Manchester M60 3XN
Tel: 0845 766 0163
Website: www.mind.org.uk
e-mail: contact@mind.org.uk

35 **Momentum Scotland** *(Vocational rehabilitation)*
Intercity House, 80 Oswald Street, Glasgow G1 4PL
Tel: 0141 221 2333
Website: www.momentumscotland.org
e-mail: headoffice@momentumscotland.org

36 **National Back Exchange**
Administration Office, Plantation House,
The Bell Plantation, Watling Street, Towcester,
Northants NN12 6HN
Tel: 01327 358855
Website: www.nationalbackexchange.org.uk
e-mail: nationalbackexch@btconnect.com

37 **National Society for Epilepsy**
Chesham Lane, Chalfont St Peter,
Buckinghamshire SL9 0RJ
National Epilepsy Helpline: 01494 601400
Website: www.epilepsynse.org.uk

38 **Repetitive Strain Injury Association**
380-384 Harrow Road, London W9 2HU
RSI Helpline: 0800 018 5012
Website: www.rsi.org.uk

39 **Rehab UK**
Windermere House, Kendal Avenue, London W3 0XA
Tel: 0208 896 2333
Website: www.rehab.ie/uk/ e-mail: info@rehabuk.org

40 **Royal National Institute of the Blind**
105 Judd Street, London WC1H 9NE
Helpline: 0845 766 9999
Website: www.rnib.org.uk

41 **Royal National Institute of Deaf People**
19-23 Featherstone Street, London EC1Y 8SL
Information Helpline: 0808 808 0123
Website: www.rnid.org.uk
e-mail: informationline@rnid.org.uk

42 **Royal Association for Disability and Rehabilitation**
12 City Forum, 250 City Road, London EC1V 8AF
Tel: 020 7250 3222
Website: www.radar.orgco.uk
e-mail: radar@radar.org.uk

43 **Shaw Trust** *(Advice, eg on retaining ill and disabled employees)*
Shaw House, Epsom Square, White Horse Business Park, Trowbridge, Wiltshire BA14 0XJ
Tel: 01225 716350
Website: www.shaw-trust.org.uk
e-mail: stir@shaw-trust.org.uk

44 **Spinal Injuries Association**
Suite J, 3rd Floor, Acorn House, 387-391
Midsummer Boulevard, Milton Keynes, MK9 3HP
Tel: 0800 980 0501
Website: www.spinal.co.uk
e-mail: sia@spinal.co.uk

Appendix 5  Organisations that can provide further advice

## Employer, employee and insurers' associations

45  **Association of British Insurers**
51 Gresham Street, London, EC2V 7HQ
Tel: 020 7600 3333
Website: www.abi.org.uk
e-mail: info@abi.org.uk

46  **Association of Personal Injury Lawyers**
11 Castle Quay, Nottingham NG7 1FW
Tel: 0115 958 0585
Website: www.apil.com
e-mail: receptionist@apil.com

47  **The Rehabilitation Working Party**
c/o Anthony Dickinson,
International Underwriting Association,
London Underwiting Centre, 3 Minister Court,
Mincing Lane, London EC3R 7DD
email: anthony.dickinson@iua.co.uk

48  **Confederation of British Industry**
Centre Point, 103 New Oxford Street,
London WC1A 1DU
Website: www.cbi.org.uk

49  **EEF, the manufacturers' organisation**
Broadway House, Tothill Street, London SW1H 9NQ
Tel: 020 7222 7777
Website: www.eef.org.uk
e-mail: enquiries@eef-fed.org.uk

50  **Employers' Organisation for local government**
Diversity, Health and Safety and Pensions Division,
Layden House, 76-86 Turnmill Street,
London EC1M 5LG
Tel: 020 7296 6600
Website: www.lg-employers.gov.uk
e-mail: eo-comms@lg-employers.gov.uk

51  **Trades Union Congress**
Congress House, Great Russell Street,
London WC1B 3LS
Tel: 020 7636 4030
Website: www.tuc.org.uk
e-mail: info@tuc.org.uk

52  **Northern Ireland Committee, Irish Congress of Trade Unions**
3 Crescent Gardens, Belfast BT7 1NS
Tel: 028 9024 7940
Website: www.ictuni.org
e-mail: info@ictuni.org

53  **Scottish Trades Union Congress**
333 Woodlands Road, Glasgow G3 6NG
Tel: 0141 337 8100
Website: www.stuc.org.uk
e-mail: info@stuc.org.uk

54  **Wales Trades Union Congress Cymru**
1 Cathedral Road, Cardiff CF11 9SD
Tel: 02920 347 010
Website: www.wtuc.org.uk
e-mail: wtuc@tuc.org.uk

## Health professional associations

55  **Association of Chartered Physiotherapists in Occupational Health and Ergonomics**
The Cottage, Hornsea Road, Atwick, Driffield,
East Yorkshire YO25 8DG
Tel: 0196 453 4376
E-mail: jslsda@aol.com

56  **British Chiropractic Association**
Blagrave House, 17 Blagrave Street, Reading,
Berkshire RG1 1QB
Tel: 0118 950 5950
Website: www.chiropractic-uk.co.uk
e-mail: enquiries@chiropractic-uk.co.uk

57  **British Society of Rehabilitation Medicine**
c/o Royal College of Physicians,
11 St Andrews Place, London NW1 4LE
Tel: 01992 638865
Website: www.bsrm.co.uk
e-mail: admin@bsrm.co.uk

58  **Case Management Society UK**
PO Box 2073, Reading RG4 7ZJ
Tel: 0118 948 2272
Website: www.cmsuk.org
e-mail: info@cmsuk.org

# Appendix 5  Organisations that can provide further advice

59  **Chartered Society of Physiotherapy**
Headquarters, 14 Bedford Row, London WC1R 4ED
Tel: 0207 306 6666
Website: www.csp.org.uk

60  **College of Occupational Therapists**
106-114 Borough High Street, Southwark,
London SE1 1LB
Tel: 0207 357 6480
Website: www.cot.co.uk

61  **Commercial Occupational Health Providers Association**
PO Box 6873, Wellingborough, NN8 1ZP
Tel: 01933 227788
Wesbite: www.cohpa.co.uk  e-mail: info@cohpa.co.uk

62  **Faculty of Occupational Medicine**
6 St Andrew's Place, London NW1 4LB
Tel: 020 7317 5890
Website: www.faococcmed.ac.uk
e-mail: fom@facoccmed.ac.uk

63  **Institute of Occupational Medicine**
Research Park North, Riccarton, Edinburgh EH14 4AP
Tel: 0870 8505131
Website: www.iom-world.org
e-mail: www.info@iomhq.org.uk

64  **Organisation of Chartered Physiotherapists in Private Practice**
PhysioFirst, Cedar House, The Bell Plantation,
Watling Street, Towcester, Northants NN12 6HN
Tel: 01327 354441
Website: www.physiofirst.org.uk
e-mail: towcester@physiofirst.org.uk

65  **Scottish Chiropractic Association**
16 Jenny Moores Road, St Boswells TD6 0AL
Tel: 01835 824026
Website: www.sca-chiropractic.org
e-mail: sca.mcairn@virgin.net

66  **Society of Occupational Medicine**
6 St Andrew's Place, London NW1 4LB
Tel: 020 7486 2641
Website: www.som.org.uk
e-mail: admin@som.org.uk

## Human resources advice

67  **Chartered Institute of Personnel and Development**
CIPD House, Camp Road, Wimbledon,
London SW19 4UX
Tel: 020 8971 9000
Website: www.cipd.org.uk

## Other sources of advice

68  **Managing Sickness Absence**
Website: www.managingabsence.org.uk

69  **Working Backs Scotland Partnership**
Website: www.workingbacksscotland.com

# Appendix 6  Useful publications

## HSE priced publications

*Health surveillance at work* HSG61 (Second edition)
HSE Books 1999 ISBN 0 7176 1705 X

*Management of health and safety at work. Management of Health and Safety at Work Regulations 1999. Approved Code of Practice and guidance* L21 (Second edition)
HSE Books 2000 ISBN 0 7176 2488 9

*Manual handling. Manual Handling Operations Regulations 1992 (as amended). Guidance on Regulations* L23 (Third edition)
HSE Books 2004 ISBN 0 7176 2823 X

*Mental well-being in the workplace:
A resource pack for management training and development*
HSE Books 1998 ISBN 0 7176 1524 3

*Real solutions, real people:
A managers' guide to tackling work-related stress*
HSE Books 2003 ISBN 0 7176 2767 5

*Tackling work-related stress:
A managers' guide to improving and maintaining employee health and well-being* HSG218
HSE Books 2001 ISBN 0 7176 2050 6

*Upper limb disorders in the workplace*
HSG60 (Second edition)
HSE Books 2002 ISBN 0 7176 1978 8

## HSE free publications

### Sickness absence

*Off work sick and worried about your job? Steps you can take to help your return to work* Leaflet INDG397
HSE Books 2004 (single copy free or priced packs of 15 ISBN 0 7176 2915 5)

*Managing sickness absence and return to work in small businesses* Desk aid INDG399 HSE Books 2004 (single copy free or priced packs of 20 ISBN 0 7176 2914 7)

### General health and safety

*Consulting employees on health and safety:
A guide to the law* Leaflet INDG232
HSE Books 1996 (single copy free or priced packs of 15 ISBN 0 7176 1615 0)

*Five steps to risk assessment* Leaflet INDG163(rev1)
HSE Books 1998 (single copy free or priced packs of 10 ISBN 0 7176 1565 0)

*Managing health and safety:
Five steps to success* Leaflet INDG275
HSE Books 1998 (single copy free or priced packs of 10 ISBN 0 7176 2170 7)

*Need help on health and safety?
Guidance for employers on when and how to get advice on health and safety* Leaflet INDG322
HSE Books 2000 (single copy free or priced packs of 10 ISBN 0 7176 1790 4)

*Stating your business:
Guidance on preparing a health and safety policy document for small firms* Leaflet INDG324
HSE Books 2000 (single copy free or priced packs of 5 ISBN 0 7176 1799 8)

*Understanding ergonomics at work:
Reduce accidents and ill health and increase productivity by fitting the task to the worker* Leaflet INDG90(rev2)
HSE Books 2003 (single copy free or priced packs of 15 ISBN 0 7176 2599 0)

*Understanding health surveillance at work:
An introduction for employers* Leaflet INDG304
HSE Books 1999 (single copy free or priced packs of 15 ISBN 0 7176 1712 2)

*Using work equipment safely* Leaflet INDG229(rev1)
HSE Books 2002 (single copy free or priced packs of 10 ISBN 0 7176 2389 0)

*Tax rules and the purchase of occupational health support* (available from the HSE website only)

# Appendix 6 Useful publications

*Drugs and alcohol*
*Don't mix it:*
*A guide for employers on alcohol at work* Leaflet INDG240 HSE Books 1996 (single copy free or priced packs of 10 ISBN 0 7176 1291 0)

*Drug misuse at work:*
*A guide for employers* Leaflet INDG91(rev2)
HSE Books 1998
(single copy free or priced packs of 10 ISBN 0 7176 2402 1)

*Musculoskeletal disorders*
*Aching arms (or RSI) in small businesses:*
*Is ill health due to upper limb disorders a problem in your workplace?* Leaflet INDG171(rev1)
HSE Books 2003 (single copy free or priced packs of 15 ISBN 0 7176 2600 8)

*Getting to grips with manual handling: A short guide* Leaflet INDG143(rev2) HSE Books 2004 (single copy free or priced packs of 15 ISBN 0 7176 2828 0)

*In the driving seat: Advice to employees on reducing back pain in drivers and machinery operators* Leaflet INDG242 HSE Books 1997 (single copy free or priced packs of 10 ISBN 0 7176 1314 3)

*Manual handling assessment charts* Leaflet INDG383
HSE Books 2003 (single copy free or priced packs of 10 ISBN 0 7176 2741 1)

*Working with VDUs* Leaflet INDG36(rev2)
HSE Books 2003 (single copy free or priced packs of 10 ISBN 0 7176 2222 3)

*Stress*
*Work-related stress: A short guide* Leaflet INDG281(rev1)
HSE Books 2001 (single copy free or priced packs of 10 ISBN 0 7176 2112 X)

**Free leaflets downloadable from HSENI website**
*Backworks Northern Ireland: A leaflet for employers and workers in business* HSENI 2003

*Balancing disability rights and health and safety requirements: A guide for employers* HSENI 2002

*Guidelines on developing and implementing workplace drugs and alcohol policies* HSENI 2003

## Other publications (see Appendix 5 for organisation contact details)

**Bodily Injury Claims Management Association**
*The Rehabilitation Code* (downloadable from www.bicma.org.uk)

**Department of Trade and Industry**
*Individual rights of employees: A guide for employers and employees* PL716 (Rev10)
DTI 2003 (downloadable information)

**Disability Rights Commission**
*The Disability Discrimination Act 1995: Code of Practice on Employment and Occupational Health*
(downloadable information)

**EEF, the manufacturers' organisation**
*Fit for work: The complete guide to managing sickness absence and rehabilitation* The Engineering Employers Federation 2004 ISBN 1903461375

**Employers' Forum on Disability**
*Retaining your Workforce* Employers' Forum on Disability 2004

*Unlocking the Evidence: The New Disability Business Case* Employers' Forum on Disability 2001 ISBN 0 90389 401 8

**Employers' Organisation for local government**
*Management of Ill Health Handbook*
Employers' Organisation for local government 2002
ISBN 0 74889 225 7

**Faculty of Occupational Medicine**
*Back pain at work: A guide for people at work and their employers* Faculty of Occupational Medicine 2000

*Guidance on Ethics for Occupational Physicians* (5th Edition) Faculty of Occupational Medicine 1999 ISBN 1 86016 112 X

**Information Commissioner's Office**
*The Employment Practices Data Protection Code*
Information Commissioner's Office 2002

**Inland Revenue**
*What to do if your employee is sick*
E14 Inland Revenue 2004

*What to do if your employee is sick: Special cases*
E14 Supplement Inland Revenue 2004

## Appendix 6 Useful publications

*National Institute for Mental Health in England*
*Line manager's resource: A practical guide to managing and supporting mental health in the workplace*
Department of Health 2001 (downloadable information). Also available free of charge from 0870 443 0930 or mindout@codestorm.co.uk

*The Stationery Office*
*The Back Book: The best way to deal with back pain. Get back active* (2nd Edition)
The Stationery Office 2002 ISBN 0 11 702949 1

*The Whiplash Book: How you can deal with a whiplash injury. Based on the latest medical research*
The Stationery Office 2002 ISBN 0 11 702862 2

HSE priced and free publications are available by mail order from HSE Books, PO Box 1999, Sudbury,
Suffolk CO10 2WA
Tel: 01787 881165
Fax: 01787 313995
Website: www.hsebooks.co.uk (HSE priced publications are also available from bookshops and free leaflets can be downloaded from HSE's website: www.hse.gov.uk.)

For information about health and safety ring HSE's Infoline
Tel: 08701 545500
Fax: 02920 859260
e-mail: hseinformationservices@natbrit.com or write to HSE Information Services, Caerphilly Business Park, Caerphilly CF83 3GG.

The Stationery Office (formerly HMSO) publications are available from The Publications Centre,
PO Box 276, London SW8 5DT
Tel: 0870 600 5522
Fax: 0870 600 5533
Website: www.tso.co.uk (They are also available from bookshops.)

# References

This guide draws on research evidence as follows.

**The general evidence base for the guide is contained in specially commissioned research**
*Job retention and vocational rehabilitation: The development and evaluation of a conceptual framework* RR106
HSE Books 2003 ISBN 0 7176 2204 5 (HSE Research Reports are downloadable free from the HSE website)

**'Work….is essential to health and well being' (paragraph 3)**
Brenner M H *Employment and Public Health. Volume 1: Final Report to the European Commission Directorate General: Employment, Industrial Relations and Social Affairs* 2001 DG EMPL/A/1. VC 2001/0024

*Vocational rehabilitation: The way forward* (Second edition)
British Society of Rehabilitation Medicine 2003
ISBN 0 9540879 2 5

*Employment opportunities and psychiatric disability*
CRIII Royal College of Psychiatrists 2002

Schneider J 'Work interventions in mental health care: Some arguments and recent evidence' *Journal of Mental Health* 1998 **7** (1) 81-94

**'Inability to get back to work due to poor health brings on more health problems…' (paragraph 3)**
Acheson D *Independent Inquiry into Inequalities in Health Report* The Stationery Office 1998
ISBN 0 11 322173 8

**'Companies in both the UK and USA have made significant savings ….'(paragraph 4)**
*Costs and Benefits of Return to Work and Vocational Rehabilitation in the UK*
Association of British Insurers 2004

**'The significance of social and work-related barriers to return to work and the need for employers to address these' (paragraph 10)**
Waddell G, Burton A K, Bartys S *Concepts of Rehabilitation for the Management of Common Health Problems*
The Stationery Office 2004 ISBN 0 11 703394 4

**'Examples of advice about stress-related illness eg contact with employees suffering from depression or stress-related illness' (paragraph 30)**
*Best practice in rehabilitating employees following absence due to work-related stress* RR138
HSE Books 2003 ISBN 0 7176 2715 2 (HSE Research Reports are downloadable free from the HSE website)

# Managing sickness absence and return to work

## An employers' and managers' guide

Sickness absence can have a big impact on the productivity of your business and the life of your workers. If not managed effectively it can have devastating effects on business costs and the quality of life of the employee concerned.

This guide is for managers and employers. It shows best practice and also offers simple, practical advice and suggests steps you can take to help employees following injury, ill health or the onset of disability. It aims to help you reduce sickness absence, improve competitiveness and the productivity of your business, as well as protecting the well-being of your employees. It will also be helpful to trade union and other employee representatives.

This book:
- takes you through the steps to helping people back to work;
- provides advice on workplace and external factors that can act as barriers to successful return to work;
- offers suggestions on developing a company or organisational return to work policy;
- gives advice on preventing risks to the health and safety of ill, injured or disabled employees;
- lists other sources of help and information.

£9.95

ISBN 0-7176-2882-5

9 780717 628827

HSG249